How to Play Golf for Kids

The Ultimate Guide to Learning, Playing, and Becoming Proficient at the Sport

© Copyright 2023 - All rights reserved.

The content contained within this book may not be reproduced, duplicated, or transmitted without direct written permission from the author or the publisher.

Under no circumstances will any blame or legal responsibility be held against the publisher, or author, for any damages, reparation, or monetary loss due to the information contained within this book, either directly or indirectly.

Legal Notice:

This book is copyright protected. It is only for personal use. You cannot amend, distribute, sell, use, quote, or paraphrase any part of the content within this book without the consent of the author or publisher.

Disclaimer Notice:

Please note the information contained within this document is for educational and entertainment purposes only. All effort has been executed to present accurate, up-to-date, reliable, and complete information. No warranties of any kind are declared or implied. Readers acknowledge that the author is not engaging in the rendering of legal, financial, medical, or professional advice. The content within this book has been derived from various sources. Please consult a licensed professional before attempting any techniques outlined in this book.

By reading this document, the reader agrees that under no circumstances is the author responsible for any losses, direct or indirect, that are incurred as a result of the use of the information contained within this document, including, but not limited to, errors, omissions, or inaccuracies.

Table of Contents

Introduction 1

Chapter 1: Understanding and Background to Golf 3

Chapter 2: Getting Started with Golf 14

Chapter 3: The Golf Swing... 26

Chapter 4: Putting and Short Game 38

Chapter 5: Playing on the Course 48

Chapter 6: Golf Skills and Drills.................................... 57

Chapter 7: Staying Safe and Healthy 68

Chapter 8: The Joy of Golf...78

Conclusion 86

References 88

Introduction

If you're a child curious about the exciting world of golf, you've come to the right place. This book is your ultimate guide to getting started on the greens and having fun.

What's the Purpose?

This book introduces you to the beautiful game of golf so that it's easy to understand. Learning something new can be tricky. Don't worry. This book has got you covered. The book aims to ensure that every child can pick up a club, hit the ball, and enjoy every swing of the game.

What Makes It Different?

Child-Friendly Language: The book uses simple words and clear explanations so you will know golf jargon.

Step-by-Step Instructions: Everything is broken down into easy-to-follow steps. You'll find clear, hands-on instructions to help you master each skill, from holding the club to sinking a perfect putt.

Lots of Pictures: A picture is worth a thousand words. The book is packed with colorful illustrations showing you exactly what to do. You'll understand the techniques and tricks easily.

Fun Games and Tips: Learning golf is incredible. It's even better when it's fun. Exciting games and tips are included to keep you engaged and eager to get on the golf course.

Safety First: You'll not only learn to play golf but also how to play it safely. You'll learn the rules and etiquette that make golf a respectful and enjoyable sport.

So, keep reading if you're ready to embark on an incredible golfing adventure.

Chapter 1: Understanding and Background to Golf

Before diving in, understanding what golf is all about is essential. It's a fantastic sport played on a giant playground called a golf course. It's a game of skill, patience, and precision. The game aims to strike the ball into a small hole in as few tries as possible. Sounds simple, right? It can be tricky, but that's where the fun comes in.

1. *Golf is a game of skill, patience, and precision. Source: https://www.pexels.com/photo/golf-ball-in-close-up-photography-6572957/*

Most outdoor golf courses are filled with trees, obstacles, and lush, green, neatly trimmed grass. Each golf course has a unique landscape explicitly designed by golf course architects. Golf courses have different areas labeled as "fairways," "greens," and "bunkers," and each spot has its purpose.

The Golf Course

Imagine the golf course as a vast, beautiful park with grass, trees, and sometimes ponds, sand pits, and uncut grass. It's on the golf course where all the action happens. As mentioned, areas are divided into sections, like fairways, greens, and bunkers, with unique roles. Here's what these sections represent:

Tee: Consider the tee as a special starting place for each hole. It's the area where you will make your first strike.

Fairway: After you hit your ball from the tee, you'll find yourself on the fairway, a long, grassy path leading you closer to the hole. The grass here is neatly cut, making it easier to hit the ball and have more control over the strike.

Green: The green is a small area with finely cut grass. Consider it as the finish line of each golf hole. The terrain on the green is even, with some elevated or sunken areas. Nonetheless, you'll use the putter to strike the ball gently, so it goes into the hole.

Bunker: These are primarily sand-filled areas intentionally designed to test the golfers' skills. Most players struggle to get the golf ball out of the sand and back onto the fairway or green.

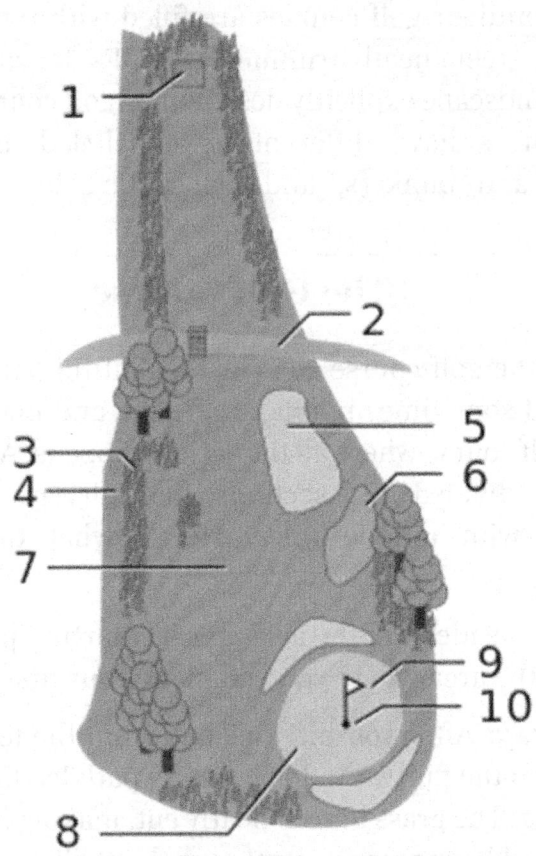

2. It's on the golf course where all the action happens. Source: Totatarouderivative work: R. Engelhardt (talk, contribs, Gallery) (German Wikipedia)derivative work: Beao, CC BY-SA 3.0 <http://creativecommons.org/licenses/by-sa/3.0/>, via Wikimedia Commons: https://commons.wikimedia.org/wiki/File:Golf_field.svg

The Golf Tools

Like any sport, you need equipment and gear. Here are the essentials you should get before hitting the golf course:

Golf Clubs: Clubs are like extremely long magic wands with which you hit the ball. A golf club set comprises a variety of clubs, each serving a different purpose and situation. For example, iron clubs cover short distances, the driver is always picked for long shots, and a putter gently strikes the ball, so it falls into the hole.

Golf Balls: Gold balls are small, hard, and covered in tiny bumps. When you hit them with your clubs, these bumps help them fly through the air smoothly. While the outside is solid, the inner comprises three core layers, each made from rubber with different properties.

Golf Bag: The golf set you purchase comes in a bag that not only carries the clubs securely but also provides space to store golf balls, tees, and other equipment that might be required in-game.

Golf Tee: The tee is what you put the golf ball on, elevating it from the ground and making it easier to hit.

Now that you have had a quick introduction, it's time to start your golfing adventure. It's time to dig deeper into the exciting world of golf in the coming chapters. So, get ready to tee off and have loads of fun.

The History of Golf

Golf's roots extend back hundreds of years in Scotland. Back then, people used wooden sticks to hit poorly crafted balls to hit stones, ground targets, or self-made rabbit holes. It was the initial stage of the game known today as Golf. The game evolved from using sticks and crude material to playing in outclass golf courses with state-of-the-art equipment.

Simple Equipment

The early golfers didn't have today's fancy clubs and golf balls. They used simple things like wooden sticks to hit the ball. The balls were made of leather and stuffed with feathers. Like golf today, it was about figuring out how to get the ball into the hole using as few strokes as possible.

Creating Golf Courses

As more people started playing golf, they needed more prominent places. So, they made particular areas called golf courses. These courses had several holes, and players would move from one hole to another, just as they do today. Nowadays, golf courses are not limited to the outdoors. Technologies like virtual reality (VR) and augmented reality (AR) are primarily used to play indoors, but the true spirit of the game lies out there under the blue sky.

Rules and Special Names

Coming back to history, eventually, people created golf rules to ensure everyone played fairly. They gave unique names to each part of the golf course, like "tee," which is where you start, "fairway," the long, grassy part, and "green," where the hole is. These names helped golfers understand what to do at each part of the course.

Famous Golfers

As time went on, golfers became good at the game, and tournaments were established. They won essential golf tournaments like the Masters and the Open Championship. These golfers became famous and inspired many enthusiasts to take up golf.

Golf Today

Today, people of all ages play golf worldwide: high-tech golf clubs, colorful golf balls, and beautiful golf courses with neatly trimmed grass are available to practice. Besides golf clubs, there are plenty of golf ranges where players can fine-tune their strokes. People from different countries play together, having fun, making new friends, and enjoying the fresh air outdoors.

So, that's the long and fascinating history of golf. It started with simple sticks and balls in Scotland and grew into the fantastic game we know today. You can become a famous golfer one day, so keep practicing and having fun on the golf course.

Why Children Should Play Golf

It's Great Exercise

Golf is a sport involving much walking and swinging, so you're moving around a lot when you're on the golf course. All the walking is excellent exercise for your legs and helps keep your heart healthy. You strengthen your muscles when you swing the golf club to hit the ball. Hence, golf is a sneaky way to stay fit while having fun outdoors. Combining golf with pre-game stretching exercises and taking adequate rest after the game will keep the body physically fit and boost your immune system and defenses against potential diseases and infections.

Spending Time Outdoors

Being outside in the fresh air and sunshine is excellent for your health. You feel happier, less stressed, and more relaxed. Moreover, you get to enjoy the beauty of nature while you play. It's a healthy activity when done the right way.

3. Being outside in the fresh air and sunshine is excellent for your health. Source: https://pixabay.com/photos/boy-piggyback-siblings-children-1846236/

Learning Patience

Golf can be tricky. Sometimes, you don't hit the ball exactly how you want to, and that's okay. Golf teaches you to be patient. It shows you that it's okay to make mistakes because you can keep improving.

Making Friends

Golf is often played with others, like family or friends. When you play together, you can chat and have fun. You can laugh at funny moments, encourage each other, and enjoy friendly competitions. It's a great way to make new friends and share good times. Each time you hit the golf course, you'll see new faces sharing the same passion, making it easier to interact and learn new things.

Practicing Focus

Golf needs a lot of concentration. You must determine how to hit the ball just right. It helps you focus on the task better, a valuable skill for school and life. You can use it as a life skill, and apply it when studying, doing homework, or participating in quizzes.

Learning Respect

Golf has many rules and etiquette to encourage polite behavior. You learn to respect the golf course by caring for it and not making a mess. You learn to be respectful to the other players and yourself. It's about being a good sport and treating everyone equally.

Setting Goals

You have a goal for each hole. This goal is to get the ball into the hole with as few strokes as possible. It teaches you about setting and working hard to achieve goals, which are valuable life skills.

Family Fun

One of the remarkable things about golf is that it's a game that people of all ages can enjoy together. You can go to the golf course with your parents, grandparents, siblings, or cousins and have a fantastic time. It's a great way to spend time with your family and create beautiful memories.

Lifelong Hobby

You can play golf your whole life. It's not only for adults. Children and older folks play it, too. So, when you play golf, you learn skills that can bring you joy for many years.

Golf Is Fun

Golf is a whole lot of fun. Trying to hit the ball just right, watching it roll across the grass, and celebrating when it goes into the hole is a fantastic feeling. It is simultaneously an exciting and relaxing game, and why so many people love it.

Problem-Solving

Golf is like a giant puzzle. You must figure out how to get the ball into the hole using as few strokes as possible. However, you must overcome many obstacles along the way. So, playing golf helps you become a better problem solver. You'll be the one to decide which club to pick, the power and speed you will be hitting the ball with, and its angle.

Nature Exploration

Golf courses are often set in beautiful natural surroundings, and you get to explore these places when you play. You might see birds, squirrels, or even frogs near the ponds. It's a chance to connect with nature and appreciate the outdoors.

Healthy Competition

Golf can be competitive but in a friendly way. You have a chance to challenge yourself and improve your skills when you play with others. Healthy competition teaches you to set goals, work hard, and handle winning and losing graciously.

Hand-Eye Coordination

Golf entails accurately hitting the ball, which requires good hand-eye coordination. This skill can help you in other activities, like playing other sports, drawing, or playing musical instruments.

Mental Toughness

Golf can be a test of mental strength. It's a game where you must stay calm and focused, especially when unplanned things happen. Staying cool under pressure is an essential life skill you can learn from golf. Losing your temper when failing to play the perfect stroke will only worsen the gameplay outcomes. You won't be able to focus and make calculated moves.

Travel Opportunities

Golf is played worldwide. You can travel to different places to play in tournaments or with new friends as you improve your game. It's a great way to explore different cultures and make golf buddies.

Time with Family

Golf is a sport many families enjoy together. When golfing with your family, you get to spend quality time together, away from screens and distractions. It's a chance to bond and have fun as a family.

4. *Golf is a sport many families enjoy together. Source: https://pixabay.com/photos/frogs-athletes-soccer-tennis-golf-1213652/*

Career Opportunities

Some players become professional golfers when they grow up and can earn a living playing golf. Even if you don't become a pro, knowing how to play golf can be helpful in many careers. Golf is often used as a venue for business meetings and networking.

Personal Achievement

Each time you play, you can improve and achieve your best. Celebrating your achievements, whether hitting a great shot or getting your best score, feels fantastic and boosts self-confidence.

Timeless Tradition

Golf is a sport that has been loved for generations. By playing golf, you're joining a long and rich tradition and becoming a member of a club with a unique history.

Playing golf isn't only about hitting a ball. It's about having adventures, learning essential life skills, and staying healthy. Start with learning the basics of the game and the rules you must follow, get proper equipment, and start practicing. If you face difficulty striking the ball effectively, you might need to take introductory lessons from a golf coach to work on your swing and posture.

So, grab your golf clubs, put on your favorite hat, and head to the golf course for some awesome fun.

Chapter 2: Getting Started with Golf

Golf is not only for grown-ups in funny-looking pants. Nope, it's a sport about swinging big sticks, chasing little white balls, and having a blast at the same time. This chapter is your ultimate guide to the golf basics. If you've ever wondered what golfers are up to on the lush green fields or why they call it a "birdie" when no birds are involved, you're in the right place. Hold your horses, though, or more appropriately, hold your golf carts.

You must know a few things before you start whacking golf balls into the horizon. First, you must learn golf basics. Then, choosing the right equipment to hit the course like a pro is important. Also, be aware of golf etiquette because this game is about being a courteous player. So, grab your cap and shades. It's time to swing for the stars.

Choosing the Right Clubs

Golf is like a puzzle. Your golf clubs are the pieces fitting together to create the perfect swing. Imagine trying to solve a puzzle with pieces too big or too small. It wouldn't work, right? So, selecting the right golf clubs for children is like finding your secret weapon on the golf course.

Golf might seem like a complicated game at first. It requires a coordinated body movement like a choreographed dance but with a golf club instead of fancy footwork. The golf swing is a little like magic. It combines several muscle movements, like a twist here, a turn there, and a swoosh at just the right moment. You need strong, flexible muscles, especially in your upper and lower body, and excellent hand-eye coordination to make that ball sail straight and true.

So, your golf clubs should be tailor-made for you. They should feel like an extension of your arms as if they were made only for you. Hence, the golf clubs' length and weight are crucial.

5. *Your golf clubs should be tailor-made for you. Source: https://www.pexels.com/photo/a-woman-holding-a-golf-club-while-walking-9207390/*

1. Length Matters

Imagine trying to eat ice cream with a spoon too long or too short. It would be a mess. The same goes for golf clubs. If your club is too long, it might be challenging to control your swing. If it's too short, you won't have enough power. So, finding the perfect golf club's length for you is crucial.

2. Weighty Decisions

Golf clubs come in all shapes and sizes, and their weights vary, too. A golf club that's too heavy can make your swing feel like lifting a giant boulder. A club that's too light might feel like you're swinging a feather. You want that perfect balance, not too heavy, not too light: just perfect.

So, how do you find the perfect golf club match?

1. Measure Up

Grab a grown-up and a measuring tape, and measure your height. Your height is your golf club compass. It'll help you figure out the right length for your clubs.

2. Swing Test

Visit a local golf shop or golf course with a practice range. Try a few clubs and see which one feels most comfortable when you swing. Remember, it should feel like an extension of you – smooth and easy.

3. Ask the Pros

Don't be afraid to ask the pros for advice. They've been around the golf course a few times and can help you find the perfect fit. They might have cool tips and tricks to share.

4. Try before You Buy

Before you commit to a set of clubs, try them out on the golf course. It's like test-driving a car before buying it. They must feel right when you're in action.

5. Be Patient

Finding the perfect golf club might take time. But remember, even the best golfers started somewhere, and practice makes perfect.

In golf, various clubs are for different situations, like drivers for those big, powerful shots, irons for more controlled shots, and putters for those smooth, precise strokes on the green. As a beginner, you might start with a simple set, including a driver, a few irons, and a putter. Here's a pro tip: As you grow and become a better golfer, your clubs will also need an upgrade. Like you outgrow your favorite sneakers, you will outgrow your golf clubs. That's okay. It means you're getting better and stronger.

Other Equipment

Getting the perfect golf clubs will indeed make or break your game, but other equipment is just as necessary. Consider these:

- **Golf Balls**: Get your hands on colorful golf balls that are easy to spot in the grass. They're perfect for practicing your swings and aiming for that hole-in-one.

- **Golf Bag**: Every young golfer needs a golf bag to carry their clubs and balls. Choose one with fun designs and comfy straps.

- **Golf Shoes:** Keep your feet happy and your swings steady with golf shoes specially made for children. They have special grips to help keep your balance on the course.

- **Gloves:** Golf gloves are a must for a good grip on the club. Look for ones that fit snugly and let you swing confidently.

- **Tees:** These little tools help you tee up your golf ball perfectly. Choose colorful tees that match your golf balls for a stylish touch.

- **Markers:** Markers are handy for marking your ball's spot on the green. You can personalize them with your name or a cool design.

- **Scorecard**: Keep track of your scores with a child-friendly scorecard.

- **Hat or Cap**: Protect yourself from the sun and look sporty with a golf hat or cap. It keeps the sun out of your eyes so you can focus on your game.

- **Sunglasses:** Don't forget your shades. They make you look cool and shield your eyes from the sun.

6. *Every young golfer needs a golf bag to carry their clubs and balls. Source: https://www.pexels.com/photo/golf-equipment-on-grassy-field-7758346/*

Golf Etiquette for Children

Golfing etiquette is the golf course's secret code. Like learning any code, you must understand it before you swing your clubs like a pro.

1. Be a Polite Player

Imagine you're in a library. What do you do? You don't speak loudly, right? Well, the same goes for the golf course. No yelling or screaming allowed. Golf is a game of focus and concentration, so keep it quiet and polite.

2. Walk, Don't Run

Golf courses are big, green parks for golfers. However, running around like crazy isn't polite. So, when you're on the golf course, take it slow and steady.

3. Dress the Part

Golfers have a special dress code. Check the rules of the golf course, and dress appropriately. Golf shoes, collared shirts, and no beachwear are the general rule of thumb.

7. *Golfers have a special dress code. Source: https://www.pexels.com/photo/family-playing-golf-9207297/*

4. Be a Good Neighbor

When you're playing, there are usually other golfers on the course. Similar to sharing a playground, be mindful not to disrupt their game or make them wait too long. It's called "pace of play." It's about being considerate.

5. Love the Course

Golf courses are beautiful gardens. So, don't litter, and don't damage the course. Treat it with respect, like you would your backyard.

6. Play Fair and Square

There's a special order for taking turns in golf. Always follow this order when it's your turn to swing. It's polite and makes the game more enjoyable for everyone.

7. Don't Be a Ball Hog

Sometimes, golfers hit their balls far, and they might land close to yours. Don't pick up their balls or mess with them. It's like taking someone else's toys. Leave them and let the golfer take their next shot.

8. Stay Safe

Safety always comes first. When someone is swinging a club, stand far away so you don't accidentally get hit by the flying ball.

Remember, golf etiquette is the glue holding the game together. It makes golf more enjoyable for everyone and is a skill that will serve you well on and off the course.

Basic Rules of Golf

Golf is more than hitting a ball into a hole. It's a game of rules and strategies, making it fun and fair for everyone. The goal is to get the ball into the hole using as few shots as possible. Sounds simple, right? It's a bit trickier than it seems, but that's why it's so much fun.

9. Starting on the Right Foot: Teeing Off

Every golf adventure begins on the tee box. Similar to the starting line for a race. Here's what you need to know: Place your golf ball on a small tee (a little peg) to give it a good boost. You can find tees at the tee box.

10. Swing Time: The Golf Stroke

The swing is the coolest part of golf. It's how you hit the ball toward the hole. Here's how to do it: Stand with your feet shoulder-width apart and your knees slightly bent.

Hold the club with both hands and keep your eye on the ball.

11.   The Fairway and Rough: Where's My Ball?

Once you've hit your ball, it'll land on the fairway (nice and smooth) or the rough (an area that is a bit wild with tall grass). Knowing where your ball is helps you plan your next move. If your ball lands in the rough, use a club with more loft (a club that can lift the ball high) to get it back onto the fairway.

12.   Water Hazards: Uh-Oh, Wet Trouble

Some golf courses have water hazards, like ponds or streams. Be careful. If your ball lands in one, you might have to add a stroke to your score. So, try your best not to hit your ball into the water.

13.   Sand Traps: The Sandy Surprise

Sand traps are like big, sandy pits swallowing your ball. If your ball lands in one, get ready to use your sand wedge (a special club) to get it out. When you're in a sand trap, aim to hit the sand behind the ball, not the ball. The sand will carry the ball out of the trap.

14.   The Green: The Final Destination

The green is where the magic happens. It's where the hole is. However, you must be gentle on the green because the grass is very short. When you're on the green, tap the ball into the hole using a putter.

8. *The green is where the magic happens. Source: https://unsplash.com/photos/awin-9RBlpE*

15. Counting Strokes: Keeping Score

In golf, keeping score is counting your strokes (the number of times you hit the ball). The goal is to get the ball into the hole in as few strokes as possible. Keep track of your strokes on a scorecard, or use a golf app if you're playing on a big course.

Now that you know the basics, it's time to look at some important golfing rules:

- **No Cheating:** Honesty is highly recommended in golf. Don't cheat by moving your ball or not counting your strokes correctly. It's more fun when everyone plays fair.

- **Keep up the Pace**: Don't take too long on each shot. If you're taking too many swings or looking for a lost ball, it slows down the game for others. Move along and keep the pace going.

- **The Flagstick:** On the green, you'll see a flagstick in the hole. When you're putting it in, you can choose to leave the flagstick in or take it out. It's your choice.

- **Playing Order:** Golf has a special order for taking turns. The golfer whose ball is farthest from the hole goes first. So, be patient and wait for your turn.

- **Finish Strong**: After you've tapped the ball into the hole, finish the hole by picking up the flagstick and putting it back in the hole if you choose to remove it.

- **Play Where It Lies:** You must play the ball where it lands, even if it's in a tricky spot. Never move the ball closer to the hole.

Example Scenario 1: The Water Hazard Dilemma

Say your ball lands near a pond. You attempt to hit it over the pond to get closer to the hole. Oops. Your ball splashes into the water. What do you do?

- You must take a penalty stroke (add one to your score).
- Drop the ball near the edge of the water hazard.
- Now, you can hit the ball onto the fairway.
- Remember, it's all part of the game. Sometimes, even the best golfers hit their balls into the water.

Example Scenario 2: Lost in the Rough

Your ball has landed in the rough area with tall, wild grass on the side of the fairway. You can't see your ball anywhere. What's the rule?

- You must take a one-stroke penalty (add one to your score).

- Drop another ball where you think the first one went into the rough.

- Now, you can hit the ball back onto the fairway.

- It's an adventure in the grass to find your ball.

Golf might seem tricky at first, but with practice and knowing the rules, you'll soon become an amazing golfer. So, remember to be safe, play fair, and have a blast on the golf course. Golf is a game of skill, strategy, and, most importantly, fun. Now that you have the basics down, you'll move on to learning all the neat strategies and skills to become a pro. So, keep reading.

Chapter 3: The Golf Swing

This chapter explores one of the most important aspects of playing golf: the golf swing. Think of your golf swing as the key to unlocking success on the golf course. The golf swing can be broken down into essential components so you can understand it step-by-step and become a skilled golfer.

9. *The way you swing your club will help you have a good game. Source: https://commons.wikimedia.org/wiki/File:Xavier_Gos%C3%A9_-_Jugant_al_golf_(Museu_d%27Art_Jaume_Morera).jpg*

Proper Stance

Place your feet shoulder-width apart, with the front foot slightly ahead of the golf ball. Likewise, stand so the club face reaches the golf ball while your arms are not fully outstretched. You might need your parents' or peers' supervision familiar with golf to practice a proper stance before taking the shot. The correct posture ensures proper spine angle, reduces the chances of muscle sprain or strain, and opens a window to play an impactful stroke.

The next step involves bending the knees slightly, as keeping them stiff makes the stroke challenging. As you bend your knees, distribute your body weight evenly on both feet. Although the weight shifts to the heels and toes during backswings and downswings, starting with even weight distribution is the best approach.

Feet Apart

Stand with your feet as wide apart as your shoulders. Find a comfortable and stable standing position.

Toes Outward

Turn your toes slightly outward, away from the target. It helps you make a good swing, like winding up a spring to make it work properly.

Balance Your Weight

Ensure your weight is balanced on both feet, like standing equally on both legs. You don't want to lean too much to one side.

10. *Find a comfortable and stable standing position. Source: https://www.pexels.com/photo/girl-playing-golf-1325679/*

Gripping the Club

Although there are several grips to pick from, keep a relaxed grip to improve the stroke's accuracy and the distance covered. The muscles must be relaxed so that it won't hinder the swing. Keep your stance natural, and don't overstretch the muscles. If you are unfamiliar with gripping the club, try holding the club like a baseball bat. Here's how you can make a baseball grip.

1. Grip the club with your left hand, curving the fingers.
2. Now place your right hand on the golf club close to your left hand.
3. The right-hand pinky finger should touch the index finger of the left hand.

Overlap or Interlock

You can let your right hand overlap your left hand's fingers, hugging each other. Or, you can interlock your right pinky finger between your left index and middle fingers, like holding hands.

You could use the overlap or interlocking grip, but it will take more practice for effective results. Each grip has pros and cons and variations. As you progress, experiment with different grips to refine your stroke.

Holding the Club

Imagine you're holding a pencil. Put your left hand on the top of the golf club's handle. Your thumb should point down the club. Hold the club firmly but not too tightly. Imagine you're holding a baby bird. You don't want to squeeze too hard (squishing the bird) or hold too loosely (the bird might fly away). Find the right balance (holding the bird gently).

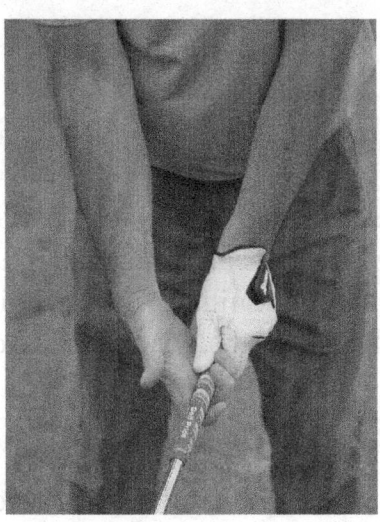

11. Hold the club firmly but not too tightly. Source: https://pixabay.com/photos/golf-correct-grip-sports-training-1452023/

Posture

Posture means how you stand and hold your body and is essential for a good golf swing. Here's what to do:

Stand Tall

Imagine a string pulling you up from the top of your head. Stand up straight and tall, like a soldier in a parade.

Bend at the Hips

Bend over at your hips, not your waist, to get closer to the ball. Similar to a polite bow.

Knees Slightly Bent

Keep your knees bent as if you're about to jump. Imagine a coiled spring. It helps you stay balanced and ready to move.

Back Straight

Keep your back straight, like a solid and sturdy wall. Don't slouch or round your back. It must be a straight line. However, don't put too much pressure on the back as it can cause inflammation of the back muscles when done incorrectly.

Relaxed Arms

Let your arms hang naturally from your shoulders. You will swing the club quickly and smoothly.

Eyes on the Ball

Always keep your eyes on the ball. Maintaining eye contact on the ball helps you hit with precision.

12. *Your posture is essential for a good golf swing. Source: https://www.pexels.com/photo/man-playing-golf-1325769/*

Swinging the Club

Backswing

The backswing is the initial position before striking the ball. You lift the club in a backswing stance, bringing it above the head. The backswing is a critical part of your golf swing. Here's a step-by-step guide to help you understand the backswing better:

Start in the Right Position

Before you begin your backswing, you must be standing perfectly. Check your grip, stance, and posture.

Turning Your Body

As you prepare for the backswing, imagine turning your body to look over your shoulder to see something behind you while keeping your eye on the ball all the time. You're turning your shoulders and hips away from where you want to hit the ball, which is the target.

Lifting the Club

As you turn your body, your golf club naturally lifts off the ground like a rocket preparing for launch. Your club should point toward the sky, ready to do its job.

Keep Your Eye on the Ball

While you're doing the backswing, always keep your eye on the golf ball. You're marking the spot of impact when the club hits the ball.

Firm Wrists

Ensure your wrists stay strong and steady. Keep them from getting floppy or wobbly. Pretend your wrists are a strong bridge that doesn't move.

Coil Like a Spring

Think of your body as a spring that's winding up. The more you turn your shoulders and hips, the more energy you store.

Take It Slow

Don't rush your backswing. Imagine pulling back a slingshot slowly before you let go. Going too fast makes it difficult to control where the ball goes.

Top of the Backswing

When you can't turn your body any farther, that's the top of your backswing. Your golf club should be pointing up, and your body should be coiled like a spring, ready to bounce. However, remember not to put too much pressure on the muscles while performing a backswing, as this can lead to muscle strain.

Pause for a Second

Pause quickly at the top of your backswing. It prepares you for the downswing, the next part of your golf swing adventure.

The Downswing

The downswing is like the exciting part of a roller coaster ride when you start going down. It's when you unleash all the energy you've stored from your backswing. Here's how to do it:

Start the Movement

After you've completed your backswing, it's time to start the downswing. Imagine pressing the "go" button on a race car.

Hips and Shoulders Together

Your hips and shoulders should turn together as you begin the downswing. They're a team working together to get things moving.

Speed and Power

You need speed and power as you swing down. This helps you hit the ball with strength and send it flying. Depending on the objective, you can control the speed and power of the swing, so the ball covers a certain distance on the golf course.

Keep Your Eye on the Ball

Don't take your eye off the ball as you start your downswing just as you did during the backswing. The ball is your target. You must ensure you hit it perfectly.

Square the Clubface

As you swing down, make sure the front part of the golf club (the clubface) meets the ball squarely (giving the ball a perfect high-five).

Follow through to the Finish

The downswing isn't the end. It's the middle part of the swing. After you hit the ball, your swing continues. Keep swinging the club down and around like you're finishing a graceful dance move.

The Follow-through

The follow-through is the continuation of the swing, guiding the ball in the right direction. It's where you put the finishing touch on your golf swing. Here's how it works:

Keep the Swing Going

As you finish the downswing, your golf club should keep moving.

High Finish

Swing the club high and over your body. Your club should point towards your target.

Balanced Finish

At the end of the follow-through, remain balanced and steady, like a statue. It helps you control where the ball goes and prevents you from tumbling over. You might face issues maintaining posture and balance on the golf course, but it will improve the more you play.

Stay Relaxed

Keep your body and arms relaxed during the follow-through. Don't force the follow-through. You might add too much strength or weight to the stroke.

Watch Your Shot

Watch the ball as it flies through the air after your follow-through. Imagine watching a shooting star streak across the sky, following its path with your eyes.

Here are additional points to consider as you practice your golf swing:

Breathing

Pay attention to your breathing. Take a deep breath before you start your swing, and exhale smoothly as you downswing and follow through. Proper breathing helps you relax and focus. You can perform regular deep breathing exercises to gain more control over your breath while playing.

Rhythm and Timing

Your swing should have a natural rhythm and timing. Keep a consistent pace throughout your swing, avoiding sudden rushes or pauses. Rushing it too much or pausing while swinging won't lead to an impactful strike.

Practice Short Swings

In addition to full swings, practice short swings like chips and pitches. These are essential for getting the ball closer to the hole on the green.

Chipping and Putting

Chipping and putting are crucial parts of the game. Practicing them can save you strokes. Think of chipping as a delicate touch, like painting fine details, and putting as precision, like aiming a dart.

13. Keep swinging the club down and around like you're finishing a graceful dance move. Source: https://pixabay.com/photos/golf-golfed-sunset-sports-golfer-787826/

Course Etiquette

Learn the rules and etiquette of golf. Be respectful to other players by staying quiet when they're swinging, fixing ball marks on the green, and keeping pace with the group ahead. Golf is not only about skill but also about good sportsmanship.

Stay Positive

Golf can be challenging, and you won't always hit perfect shots. Stay positive and focus on improving with each swing. It's a puzzle to solve rather than a test to pass.

Stay Hydrated

Drink water to stay hydrated, and apply sunscreen to protect your skin if you're playing on a sunny day. Golf can take a few hours, and you must stay comfortable throughout the game. You'll feel tired and dizzy with low energy if you don't remain well hydrated.

Have Fun

Most importantly, have fun. Golf is a game you can enjoy with friends and family. It's an adventure on a beautiful course. Enjoy the scenery and the challenge of the game. Learn from your mistakes and continue striving to improve your gameplay.

The downswing and follow-through are the grand finale of your golf swing. It's where all your hard work and preparation come together to create a beautiful shot. You can become a golfing star with a smooth downswing and graceful follow-through. So, practice these parts of your swing diligently, and you'll be on your way to becoming a fantastic golfer.

Chapter 4: Putting and Short Game

Golf is full of fancy words and tricky terms, and it can sound like school sometimes. In this chapter, you'll learn why golfers stress about the Putting and Short game and why you should, too.

Imagine this: You're on the last hole and only need one perfect swing to win. The ball lies only a couple of feet away, and as you're in a fluid motion of swinging your body to make the final strike, a world of intricate factors reveals itself. You realize it's not about the force with which you hit the ball. It's a dance with physics, timing, and strategy.

A short game is essentially understanding how this dance plays out. It's a category of shots made from within 100 yards of the green and divided into four sub-categories: putting, chipping, pitching, and greenside bunker shots. This section explains each category.

Putting Basics

What does it mean when you hear people saying the golfer is now putting the green? The golfer changes their stance. Someone's handing them a different club. You've not seen this one before, and everyone has their eyes locked on the ball, which lies only a few feet away from the winning hole. A golf putt is a low-speed stroke intended to roll the golf ball across the green into the hole or, at the very least, near the hole.

14. A golf putt is a low-speed stroke intended to roll the golf ball across the green into the hole or, at the very least, near the hole. Source: https://unsplash.com/photos/rGhgsbbWunA

Why is it such a big deal? It can make or break your game. A perfect putt can help you win the round. However, first, you must befriend the putter. It's a golf club specifically for the putting stroke. It lowers the ball's spin and ensures a smooth blow is delivered so the ball can glide gently across the grass and into the winning hole.

Proper Grip and Stance

The nitty-gritty of putting: The grip and stance are the building blocks of putting. There's no stopping you from making the perfect putt if you get them right, but you must first familiarize yourself with the proper terminology.

Top Hand

The "top hand" in golf is typically the lead hand, the hand closer to the target (in this case, the hole). For most right-handed golfers, the top hand is the left hand. For left-handed golfers, it's the right hand. If you're a right-handed golfer, your top hand would be your left hand. Likewise, if you're a left-handed golfer, your top hand would be your right hand.

The Correct Grip for Putting

Imagine you're shaking hands with a friend. It's the same pressure you should feel when putting, gentle but firm. Here's how to do it:

1. Hold the putter with both hands.
2. Your top hand should grip the putter handle so that your thumb points down its shaft and your fingers wrap comfortably around it.
3. The bottom hand supports and guides. It should grip the putter softly.

The Ideal Stance for Putting

How should you stand when putting? This part is about balance and aim:

1. Stand with your feet shoulder-width apart for a stable base.
2. Your weight should be evenly balanced on both feet, with knees slightly bent.
3. Lean forward slightly from your hips so you get closer to the ball and can see your line to the hole.

As you deliver the putt, ensure your eyes are fixated on the ball. It helps you aim straight and true.

The Putting Stroke

Putting is about the stroke. The smoother it is, the better your chances of making the winning hole. How smooth should it be? Picture a pendulum on a grandfather clock swinging back and forth with perfect regularity. That's your putting stroke, smooth and steady. Here's how to make it happen:

1. Let your arms hang down naturally and stand relaxed.
2. If you feel your elbows are locked, try rocking your shoulders back and forth.
3. Swing the putter and ensure you make smooth contact with the ball.

You'll realize your putting stroke needs a consistent beat as you practice. Find a tempo that feels right and stick with it. To help you find the perfect rhythm, consider practicing the following drill.

1. Line up balls in a row and putt them to a target, focusing on a smooth motion.
2. Use a small object, like a tee, as a target and practice getting your ball to stop near it.
3. Putt with your eyes closed to feel the rhythm without distractions.

Chipping

Chipping in golf moves the ball a short distance from the green to the hole. It looks similar to putting when executed properly. The main aim is to achieve a shorter swing by minimizing the spring and keeping it low.

15. *Chipping in golf moves the ball a short distance from the green to the hole. Source: https://unsplash.com/photos/Sv8cETYAb1Y*

Step-by-Step Chipping Technique

- **Setup**: Stand with your feet close together, about shoulder-width apart. Bend forward from the hips and let your arms hang below your shoulders. Most of your weight should be on your front foot (the one closer to the hole). This posture helps create a space, pre-setting the path through which your arms and club can swing.

- **Grip**: Hold the club with both hands close together. Your grip should be gentle but not too loose.

- **Stance:** The ball should be in the middle of your stance, not too far forward or backward. It helps you make solid contact.

- **Swing:** Use a small, controlled swing. Your arms and shoulders are the stars here, not your wrists.

- **Contact:** Focus on hitting the ball first, then the ground. This action is key to getting the ball rolling nicely toward the hole.

The best way to practice chipping is to incorporate it into your warm-up routines as you prepare for your golf game. Being a skilled chipper doesn't require immense strength or a flawless swing. You only need a little confidence when making contact with the ball.

When you excel at chipping, it becomes a valuable asset on the course. It assures you of recovering from a missed shot and reduces the pressure on your putting. This skill can level the playing field, leading to lower scores and more enjoyable rounds of golf.

Pitching

Pitching is your go-to move when you're about 40 to 50 yards away from the hole and want to get closer. Picture it as a shot with a higher trajectory and a bit more spin than chip shots, allowing you to get closer to the green.

Hitting a Basic Pitch Shot

Pitching is a gray area in golf and one of the most challenging shots to master. However, you can make it easy on yourself by practicing simplicity. Don't get caught in the web of information available, and start by perfecting your golf pitch swing. Here's how you can get started with basic pitching:

- **Remember the Three C's**: Center, center, and center. Place your weight in the middle, position the ball at the center of your stance, and align your hands and the shaft at the midpoint.
- Once your C's are in place, position your feet approximately the width of two club heads apart.
- While you swing, focus on maintaining stability in the lower part of your body.
- Strike down on the ball for precision.

If you're looking to vary the distance of your pitch shots, consider:

- Adjusting the length of your swing.
- Tweaking the tempo of your swing.
- Changing your hand placement on the club by choking down or moving up.

Pitching vs. Chipping

Pitching and chipping might look the same on the surface, but both shots exhibit distinct behaviors to how the golf ball reacts. A chip shot focuses more on rolling the golf ball, whereas a pitch shot covers a greater distance through the air than a roll.

Choosing between the two can be challenging since both shots are so alike. The choice between a pitch and a chip depends on specific terrain, which many golfers call "Reading the Green."

Reading the Green

Reading the green isn't like reading a book. There's no glossary, text, or helpful guide, and you must rely on visual cues to ensure your golf ball rolls into and not away from the winning hole.

Slope and Break of the Green

The grass is not as flat as it looks. It can hide slopes and bumps that throw your golf ball off track. To read the green, stand behind your ball and observe how the grass grows. This is called the "break." It helps you understand how the green wants to guide your ball.

Observing the Terrain

Look at the terrain carefully and see if it's higher on one side and lower on the other. It helps predict which way the ball will roll. It ensures your ball doesn't curve left or right.

Grain Matters

Grass grows in a particular direction. It's known as "grain" in golf terms. It affects your putt by slowing it down or making it go faster.

Visualize the Path

Once you've considered all the factors, it's time to visualize a path. Imagine a line from your ball to the hole, and picture the ball rolling along the line. If you have trouble visualizing, use your putter and line it up with the imaginary path. It'll help you estimate where to aim and how hard to hit the ball.

Bunker Play

Bunkers make everyone's heart race a bit faster, even if you're a pro golfer. The sandy trap gobbles up your golf ball, and its only purpose is to heighten the game's excitement. Your ball lies in the bunker when any part is in contact with the sand. You're not allowed to test the condition of the bunker, touch the sand around the ball, or make a practice swing that'll touch the sand, making it highly challenging to get your ball out of the sandy trap.

16. *The sandy trap gobbles up your golf ball, and its only purpose is to heighten the game's excitement. Source: https://www.pexels.com/photo/man-hitting-the-ball-with-a-club-in-golf-15877158/*

The Sand Wedge

When your ball detours into a bunker, you must rely on the trusty sand wedge. This club is specially designed with extra loft (the angle of the clubface) to tackle the sandy terrain. Think of it as your golf shovel, perfect for scooping the ball out of the bunker and back onto the green.

Mastering the Bunker Stance and Setup

When playing in bunkers, the correct stance can make all the difference. Imagine your feet are firmly planted in the sand, about shoulder-width apart. The tricky part is opening your clubface a little and pointing it slightly to the right (for right-handed golfers). Lean your body slightly toward the target, shifting most of your weight onto your front foot. This stance helps you scoop the ball out of the bunker.

Alternatively, you can use the splash technique by using the sand to your advantage as you hit the ball. Here's how:

1. Instead of viewing the sand as an obstacle, view it as a cushion.
2. Swing your sand wedge like a pendulum, focusing on the sand behind the ball.
3. Hit the sand a couple of inches behind the ball confidently.
4. The sand acts like a cushion, lifting the ball out and onto the green.

Distance and Trajectory

The backswing length and follow-through speed control the distance and trajectory of your bunker shots. A shorter backswing will send the ball flying high and not too far. A longer backswing with a smooth follow-through helps it travel farther.

With this newfound knowledge, head to the closest golfing course and practice your short game. From precise chipping and pitching to tackling sandy bunkers, all that is left is practice. So, grab your clubs, and don't be afraid to face challenging situations. Keep swinging, improving, and having fun on the greens.

Chapter 5: Playing on the Course

The real adventure begins as soon as you step onto the golf course. The practice range acted as your training ground, but your skills will be tested when you take the first swing of outdoor golfing.

Before diving into the nitty-gritty of playing on the course, you must know a few things. Remember, golf is a game of skill and sportsmanship. It's not only about hitting the ball until you reach the winning hole. It's about carrying yourself positively, treating others with respect, and by religiously abiding by the rules.

Etiquette is a big deal, and soon you'll realize it is not just about hitting the perfect shot. It's showing respect to your fellow players and the course. Familiarizing yourself with the game's rules ensures fair play and helps everyone have a great time. In this chapter, you'll learn to play, respect the course, and have a great time doing it.

Teeing Off

A tee shot is the first shot played from the teeing ground of a golf hole and is where your golfing adventure begins. A well-executed tee shot will set the tone for the game as you race against the course and your skills. Here's how to tee off like an expert:

17. A tee shot is the first shot played from the teeing ground of a golf hole and is where your golfing adventure begins. Source: https://www.pexels.com/photo/young-man-in-putting-position-6573256/

Tee Box

The tee box is a designated area where you place your ball to take the first shot on each hole. It is called the driving shot. The area is well-maintained to provide a level, firm surface, and its boundaries are marked by tee markers. The USGA (United States Golf Association) defines the area as a "rectangle two club-lengths deep, and the front edge is defined by the line between the forward-most points of two tee-markers set by the Committee, and the side edges defined by the lines back from the outside points of the tee-markers."

In other words, you can place your golf ball anywhere between the front of the tee markers and up to two club lengths behind them as long as it stays within the markers' width.

Tee Box Markers

You'll notice various colored tee markers, like white and even gold, on the golf course. Each color signifies a varying difficulty level. The following guide will help you familiarize yourself with the color codes.

- **Gold:** Challenging distance, primarily meant for highly skilled, low-handicap golfers.
- **Red:** Beginner-friendly, shorter distance, suitable for young golfers and newcomers.
- **White:** Intermediate level, offering a moderate challenge.
- **Blue:** Advanced level, longer distance, for experienced golfers seeking a greater challenge.
- **Black:** Expert level, the furthest distance, designed for highly skilled and low-handicap players.

While golf courses typically recognize this system, it's not set in stone. Some courses get creative with their standard tee boxes by combining multiple tees, known as combo tees. Depending on personal preferences, you can tee off from a shorter or longer distance. If you are unsure, check with your golf course's management. Some keep charts with recommended tee marker colors based on a player's average driving distance.

Selecting the Right Club

The right club can make all the difference when making your tee shot. Here's a closer look at the clubs you can use when starting your golf hole.

Driver

The driver has a big head and is perfect for hitting the ball a long way. It's like the home run hitter of your golf bag, making it great for those big, open tee shots where you want to send the ball flying as far as possible.

Wood

Woods are also good for distance but give you more control than the driver. They're the power hitters who can also hit with accuracy. So, if you want to balance distance and accuracy, woods are your friends.

Hybrids

Hybrids combine irons and wood features. These clubs offer distance but are also more forgiving, meaning they're great for young golfers who want a little extra help getting the ball where they want it to go.

Choosing the right club is hard work, but it ultimately pays off. Here are a few factors to consider before selecting the club that'll start your hole:

Distance: A wood or a hybrid can help you hit the ball far without too much trouble if you're playing on a shorter course. These clubs are turbo boosters for distance.

Comfort: Feeling comfortable with your club is essential. If one club feels more natural in your hands and gives you confidence, go with it. Golf is not only about the numbers. It's about having fun and building your skills.

Setting up Your Shot

Correctly setting up your shot lays the groundwork for winning the game. Here are the elements that make up the perfect tee shot and how you can improve them.

Stance, Grip, and Posture

Stance, grip, and posture are the holy trilogy of setting up your shot and making a strong and steady foundation. Stand with your feet about shoulder-width apart so you're balanced and ready. Your grip should be firm and your posture straight. These three things help you swing the club consistently, so you'll hit the ball more accurately.

Proper Ball Placement on the Tee

Place the ball on the tee so about half of it is above the club head when you address it. You will catch the ball on the upswing, giving you more distance and control.

Tee Height and Its Effect

Adjusting the tee's height is like adjusting a rocket's launchpad. Keep the tee high for the driver so the ball sits a bit above the club head. This lets you hit the ball on the upswing and launch it into the air. For other clubs, tee it lower so the ball sits closer to the ground, giving you more control.

Navigating the Fairway

The fairway is a golfer's best friend. It's the area between the tee box and the green where the grass is cut short and evenly, making it easier for golfers to hit their shots more accurately. This section equips you with the skills to make your fairway shots more efficient.

Club Selection for Fairway Shots

The best way to make the most of your fairway shots is to navigate confidently using the right club. Here's how to make the proper selection.

Choosing the Right Club

When you're on the fairway and planning your next shot, consider the distance to the hole. Clubs like irons or wedges are your go-to if it's a short distance. They provide accuracy and control. Fairway woods offers the right balance of distance and control for longer distances.

Yardage Markers

Yardage markers tell you how far you are from the green. Pay attention to them because they guide your club selection. If the marker says you're 150 yards away, choose a 7-iron or 6-iron. If you're closer, a pitching wedge will be more helpful. Yardage markers are your map, helping you navigate the course precisely.

Know Your Distances

Golf isn't one-size-fits-all. It's about knowing your strengths. Spend time practicing on the range to understand how far you can hit with each club. When you know your distances, you'll confidently select the best club for the shot, ensuring that you reach your target.

Hitting Fairway Shots

Precision beats power on the fairway. Here's why precision matters significantly:

Accuracy and Control over Power

When swinging your golf club on the fairway, the aim is accuracy, not sheer power. Even if you have a clear path, you must read the green, visualize the path, and, after considering all the factors, focus on hitting the ball where you want it to go. Controlled shots are your ticket to success.

Stance, Alignment, and Balance

Maintaining your form might be repetitive and tiring when golfing, but once on the course and swinging your club, you'll realize it makes a huge difference. Your posture must be correct to hit a fairway shot. Your feet should be shoulder-width apart and must align with your target. Balance is key. It ensures that you remain steady throughout your swing.

Dealing with Hazards

Befriending a golf course takes time. In the meantime, you can be aware of the potential hazards. Here are a few hazards and how to recognize and overcome them.

Bunkers

Bunkers are golf's version of a sandy beach. While you might enjoy a beach, your golf ball certainly won't. Bunkers are scattered around the course, and their primary purpose is to heighten the game's excitement, especially in tournaments. When visualizing your shots, keep an eye out for them.

Water Hazards

Golf courses double as a playing area and visually pleasing scenery where you'd want to lay a blanket and have a picnic. Some courses add water attractions like ponds and streams for aesthetic purposes. However pretty they might be, if your ball dives into one, it can be challenging to retrieve and incur costly penalties.

When you're unsure if your ball landed safely, take a penalty drop and keep the game moving. It's better to take a one-stroke penalty than risk losing your ball.

Rough

The rough is the thicker grass on the outside of the fairway. It could make your next shot more challenging, as the grass can grab your club and affect the ball's path. If your ball ends up in the rough, consider using a more lofted club to get it back on the fairway. This way, you control your shot better.

18. *If your ball ends up in the rough, consider using a more lofted club to get it back on the fairway. Source: https://pixabay.com/photos/golf-club-iron-wedge-rough-grass-881331/*

Managing Nerves on the Course

Golf can be an exciting yet nerve-wracking game, especially for beginners. Imagine you're on the golf course and about to make your first tee shot. All eyes are fixed on you, and the pressure to perform can make anyone nervous. You might need to impress your coaches or parents, and the fear of mistakes adds to the anxiety. Performing your best can seem impossible in similar scenarios. The following methods will help you stay calm, focused, and positive.

Deep Breathing

Take slow, deep breaths to calm your nerves. Slowly inhale for a count of four, hold for four, and exhale for four. Keep repeating until you feel relaxed.

Visualization

Picturing yourself making successful shots helps you stay focused and boosts confidence. It might seem silly, but it works.

Positive Self-Talk

If you struggle with negative thoughts flooding your mind before making a shot, consider replacing them with positive ones. Instead of focusing on what could go wrong, think of how it can go right. Draw from your strengths and past successes.

Have Fun

Remember, golf is a game that is meant to be enjoyable. Keep a sense of humor, smile, and enjoy the experience.

From teeing off to navigating the fairway and tackling common challenges, you've gained insights and strategies to help you become a proficient golfer in this chapter. Remember, golf is not only about hitting a ball into a hole. It's about the experience, the camaraderie, and the life lessons it offers. It's about etiquette, respect for others, and a passion for improvement.

Chapter 6: Golf Skills and Drills

By now, you've learned to swing, putt, play a short game, and everything in between. You might think, "I'm ready to hit the course and start playing." However, wait a second. You're not quite ready yet. Before you can jump into a real game, practicing the techniques you have learned and polishing your skills is crucial. This chapter will guide you. Skills and drills? That sounds serious. Don't worry. It's a lot of fun. You'll be introduced to exciting golf drills to keep you entertained while you sharpen your skills. These drills are mini-games that turn practice into play. By the end of this chapter, you'll have a toolkit of skills and drills, making you the golf pro of your group.

Practice Routines for Children

"Practice makes perfect." This is the case with golf, too. Like learning a new skill, whether playing a musical instrument or mastering a sport, practice is key. So, try these exciting golf practice routines to make you a golfing star and guarantee you loads of fun.

1. The Putting Challenge

Find a smooth and flat area on the putting green, or lay down a putting mat in your living room.

1. Start by standing about 3-5 feet away from the hole (about one big step).
2. Use your putter to tap the ball into the hole gently.
3. Attempt five putts in a row without missing. Start over if you miss.
4. Once you can do this easily, challenge yourself by moving farther from the hole.

19. *Attempt five putts in a row without missing. Source: https://www.pexels.com/photo/man-wearing-blue-shirt-playing-golf-5161913/*

2. Chipping Contest

Place a bucket, hula hoop, or a large cardboard box as your target on the green.

1. Stand about 10-15 feet away from your target.
2. Use a wedge club or a 9-iron to hit the ball into the target.
3. Keep track of how many times you can get the ball into the target in a row.
4. Try chipping from different angles when you get good at it.

3. Swing Improvement

Head to the driving range or an open area with plenty of golf balls.

1. Start with your grip. Hold the club as if you're shaking someone's hand. Not too tight and not too loose.
2. Stand with your feet shoulder-width apart and ensure that your body faces the target.
3. Swing the club back and forth smoothly. Hit the ball straight ahead.
4. Watch the ball after you hit it. Where does it go? Adjust your swing as needed.

4. Obstacle Course Golf

Create a mini-golf course in the backyard or a park using toys or cones.

1. Pretend you're on a golf adventure. Aim to get the ball through or around the obstacles.

2. Time yourself and see if you can beat your time each time you play.

5. Mini-Golf Adventure

Visit a mini-golf course with your family.

1. Mini-golf is a fun game. Each hole is a new challenge.
2. Aim to get the ball in the hole with as few shots as possible. Sometimes, you need to bounce the ball off walls, adding bigger challenges.

20. Visit a mini-golf course with your family. Source: https://www.pexels.com/photo/unrecognizable-girl-playing-golf-against-urban-building-7514005/

6. Golf Ball Hunt

Hide golf balls in your backyard or a safe area.

1. Grab a basket or a bucket, and start your golf ball treasure hunt.

2. Set a timer to see how many golf balls you can find. Can you beat your record?

7. Video Analysis

Ask an adult to record your golf swing using their smartphone or tablet.

1. Watch the video together and focus on how you stand and swing.

2. Are your feet in the right place? Is your grip like a pro's?

3. Make small changes and record again to see how you improve.

Remember, golf is about practice and having a good time. Don't get discouraged if you don't get it perfect at first. Keep practicing, keep smiling, and you'll become an amazing golfer.

Fun Games to Improve Skills

1. Golf Ball Relay Race

Get ready for a thrilling relay race while improving your golf skills.

1. Gather your friends and get into teams.

2. Each team starts at a different hole on the golf course.

3. One player from each team tees off and plays the hole, trying to get the ball in the hole in as few strokes as possible.

4. After finishing the hole, they tag the next player on their team, who goes to the next hole.

5. Keep track of your team's total strokes, and the team with the fewest strokes at the end wins the relay.

2. Fairway Accuracy Challenge

Sharpen your accuracy off the tee while aiming for the fairway.

1. Choose holes with wide fairways.

2. Before each tee shot, place a target (a hula hoop or a flag) in the fairway at a specific distance.

3. Your goal is to hit the fairway and, if possible, land your ball inside the target.

4. Collect points for hitting the fairway and bonus points for landing in the target.

5. See who can rack up the most points during your round.

3. Bunker Escape Challenge

Master the art of getting out of sand traps with style.

1. Pick a hole with a sandy bunker (sand trap).

2. Start your shot from the tee, aiming to land your ball in the bunker.

3. Once you're in the bunker, the challenge is to get out and onto the green in as few strokes as possible.

4. Try different bunker shots, like splashes (high shots) and pitches (low shots), to see which works best.

4. Putting Precision Challenge

Become a putting expert by mastering accuracy and distance control.

1. Find a flat area on the putting green.
2. Set up targets at different distances from the starting point.
3. Take turns putting toward the targets and earn points based on how close your ball gets.
4. The closer you get to the target, the more points you score.
5. Compete to see who can score the most points by the end of the challenge.

5. Golf Ball Obstacle Course

Let your creativity shine as you navigate a unique golf obstacle course.

1. Choose a hole with open space around the green.
2. Use golf bags, flags, and other equipment to create a fun obstacle course.
3. Each player takes turns chipping their ball through the obstacles and onto the green.
4. Time each player to see who can complete the course in the shortest time with the fewest strokes.

6. Golf Ball Bowling Challenge

Combine golf with bowling for a strikingly good time.

1. Pick a hole with a big, flat area near the green.
2. Set up a makeshift bowling alley using cones or flags as pins.
3. Your task is to chip your golf ball to knock down the "pins."
4. Score the game like traditional bowling and aim for strikes and spares.

7. Hole-in-One Challenge

Achieve the ultimate golf goal by scoring a hole-in-one.

1. Select a short par-3 hole not too far away.
2. Take turns trying to get your ball in the hole in just one shot.
3. Keep track of how many attempts it takes each player to make a hole-in-one.
4. Celebrate with cheers and a victory dance when someone finally makes it happen.

8. Target Flag Challenge

Enhance your approach shot accuracy and get close to the target.

1. On a par-4 or par-5 hole, place a target flag or marker at a specific distance from the green.
2. Your challenge is to hit your approach shot and land your ball as close to the target as possible.
3. Score points based on how close your ball gets to the target, with closer shots earning more points.

9. Scramble Challenge

Team up with friends and use your collective skills to conquer a hole.

1. Form teams of two or more players.
2. All teams play the same hole but start from the worst ball position among their shots.
3. Work together to get the ball in the hole with as few strokes as possible.
4. Get creative with your shots and enjoy the teamwork.

10. Golf Ball Hunt

Sharpen your ball-finding skills with this exciting challenge.

1. Play a regular round of golf, but here's the twist: Find and use only one golf ball for the entire round.
2. If you lose your ball, you're out of the challenge.
3. Stay focused on your shots and remember where your ball lands to complete the game successfully.

Building Confidence on the Course

1. Practice Makes Perfect

Practicing is like magic for getting better at golf. Spend time hitting balls at the range, practicing putting, and chipping to improve. The more you practice, the more amazing you'll become at golf.

8. Practicing is like magic for getting better at golf. Source: https://pixabay.com/photos/golf-driving-range-line-up-club-1962479/

2. Start with Easy Goals

Begin with small goals you can achieve. For instance, attempt to hit the fairway or make a certain number of putts. When you reach these goals, you'll be confident and proud.

3. Focus on the Fun, Not Only Winning

Don't worry too much about your score. Instead, focus on each step of playing golf. Think about making great swings and smart decisions. Your confidence will soar when you have fun and learn from each shot.

4. Mistakes Are OK

Everyone makes mistakes, even the pros. When you mess up, don't get upset. It's a chance to learn something new. Figure out what went wrong and use that knowledge to improve. Confidence comes from trying and learning.

5. Celebrate Your Awesome Moments

Take a moment to celebrate when you do something amazing, like reaching your goals or hitting an awesome shot. Give yourself a big high-five or a happy dance. It'll remind you how great you are and motivate you to become even better.

6. Stay Strong and Flexible

Keep your body in good shape with exercises to make you strong and flexible. Being fit helps you swing the club with power and keeps you safe from getting hurt. So, stay active and keep having fun on the golf course!

Golf is an amazingly fun game, and you can become a pro golfer someday. You don't have to wait until you're grown up to start your golf journey. Nope, you can start right now. All you have to do is practice and work on your golf skills. The more you practice, the better you'll get at hitting the ball correctly and making it go where it should. You can do amazing things when you believe in yourself and your abilities. So, as you keep practicing and improving at golf, your confidence will also grow.

Chapter 7: Staying Safe and Healthy

This chapter explores the essential topic of staying safe as a young golfer. Safety is vital when you're out on the golf course. Similar to wearing a helmet when riding your bike or looking both ways before crossing the street. The chapter covers everything you need to know to enjoy golf while keeping yourself and others safe.

The Essence of Health and Safety

Before exploring the details, understanding why health and safety are so important in golf is essential:

Protecting Yourself

Golf can be tons of fun, but it involves swinging clubs and walking long distances on a course. Protecting yourself helps prevent accidents and injuries, like avoiding tripping or getting hit by a golf ball.

Protecting Others

You're not the only one on the golf course. Other players and spectators are also within close proximity. Being safe means taking care not to harm someone else accidentally.

Enjoyment

When you're safe, you can enjoy the game fully without worrying about getting hurt.

Now that you understand why safety matters, it's time to explore how to stay safe on the golf course.

Sun Protection and Hydration

Playing golf is about swinging clubs and hitting balls. However, it's also about caring for your body, especially when you're in the sun for hours. Here's why sun protection and staying hydrated are so crucial:

21. Staying hydrated to keep your energy up and avoid feeling tired or dizzy is essential. Source: https://www.pexels.com/photo/slice-lemon-beside-glass-pitcher-on-wooden-table-3766180/

Sun Protection

The sun's heat can be intense, and spending a long time on the golf course exposes you to its rays. Too much sun can cause sunburn and skin damage, which can be uncomfortable during the game. Protect yourself by wearing sunscreen with SPF (Sun Protection Factor), a wide-brimmed hat, and sunglasses.

Stay Hydrated

Playing golf can make you sweat, especially on hot days. When you sweat, you lose water. Staying hydrated to keep your energy up and avoid feeling tired or dizzy is essential. Carry a water bottle and take sips regularly.

Seek Shade

Find shade whenever possible if it's a scorching day. Stand under a tree or use an umbrella to shield yourself from the sun. Find a cool, shady spot to rest and recharge during turns.

Sun-Protective Clothing

Consider wearing long sleeves and pants made of lightweight, sun-protective fabric. They help shield your skin from the sun while keeping you comfortable.

Hat and Sunglasses

A wide-brimmed hat protects your face and neck and keeps your head cooler. Sunglasses with UV protection shield your eyes from harmful sun rays and help you see more clearly on the course.

Avoiding Common Injuries

Golf is an enjoyable sport, but playing safely to prevent injuries is essential. Here's an in-depth look at how to stay injury-free on the golf course:

Warm Up Thoroughly

Like a car engine warms up before driving, your body needs a warm-up before golf. Spend 10-15 minutes doing gentle exercises to prepare your muscles, including light stretching, arm circles, and leg swings.

Proper Swing Mechanics

Learning the correct way to swing is paramount. Seek guidance from a coach or an experienced golfer to understand and practice proper swing mechanics. Getting your swings right improves your performance and helps prevent injuries.

Use Well-Fitted Clubs

Ensure that your golf clubs match your height and strength. Too long or heavy clubs will strain your muscles and joints, leading to discomfort and potential injuries. Similarly, shoes that fit correctly are essential for foot comfort, and the right-sized clubs are crucial for your golf game.

Mind Your Swing Intensity

Avoid trying to hit the ball with all your strength on every swing. Golf is about technique and finesse, not raw power. Overexerting can lead to muscle strain or even more severe injuries. It's akin to conserving energy during a marathon, maintaining a steady pace for consistent performance.

Back Care

Golf involves repeated twisting and bending motions. Be cautious with your back to prevent strain or injury. Lift your golf bag and clubs properly, using your legs to avoid excessive stress on your back.

Mind Your Footing

Golf courses have uneven terrain, so pay close attention to where you're walking to avoid stepping into holes or tripping over irregular ground.

Hydration Is Key

Dehydration can lead to muscle cramps, so maintaining proper hydration is vital. Carry a water bottle and take sips regularly, especially on hot days. Think of it as fueling your body to keep it running smoothly.

Respect Lightning

Lightning is a significant safety concern on golf courses because golf clubs are typically made from metal. If you see lightning or hear thunder, take it very seriously. Head indoors or seek shelter immediately and wait until it's safe to continue playing. Lightning is a powerful force of nature that should never be underestimated.

22. Lightning is a significant safety concern on golf courses because golf clubs are typically made from metal. Source: https://www.pexels.com/photo/lightning-strike-2289940/

Golf Cart Safety

If you're using a golf cart, drive it carefully and responsibly. Follow the course rules and guidelines. Avoid sudden starts, stops, or sharp turns to prevent accidents. Be respectful of other drivers and pedestrians, as you would on your bicycle, motorbike, or car.

Listen to Your Body

Pay close attention to your body during your round of golf. If something feels off, like sore muscles or discomfort, don't ignore it. Take a break, rest, and let your body recover, allowing you to return stronger.

By diligently following these safety precautions, you'll enhance your golfing experience and reduce the risk of injuries. Golf is a game that can be enjoyed for a lifetime, and staying injury-free ensures you can continue to play and improve your skills for many years.

Golf as a Lifetime Sport

One of the fantastic things about golf is it's a sport you can enjoy throughout your life. Whether you're a young golfer or well into your golden years, golf offers fun, exercise, and social connection opportunities. Here's why golf is often called a "lifetime sport" and why it can be a part of your life:

Low Impact

Golf is a low-impact sport, meaning it's gentle on your joints. Unlike high-impact activities like running, golf doesn't put excessive stress on your knees, hips, and back. It's like strolling through a beautiful park rather than sprinting on a hard track.

Physical Exercise

Walking the golf course provides excellent cardiovascular exercise. It helps keep your heart healthy and your body active. It's a refreshing hike through nature, swinging a club and hitting a ball.

Mental Challenge

Golf is not only about physical skills. It's a mental game. Planning your shots, strategizing, and staying focused challenge your brain. Your body needs physical exercise. Equally, your mind receives crucial exercise when it is focused and active.

Social Connections

Golf is a social sport that allows you to connect with friends and family and meet new people. Many lifelong, like-minded friendships are formed on the golf course. It's a gathering where everyone shares a common interest.

Continual Improvement

Golf is a sport where you can always strive for improvement. There's always something new to learn, a better shot to master, or a lower score. There will also always be someone from whom you can learn.

Adaptable to Age

Golf can be adapted to your age and physical abilities. You can modify your game to suit your needs as you age. You might use a golf cart instead of walking or choose shorter tee boxes. Golf accommodates your changing abilities like a tailor adjusts clothing to fit perfectly.

Scenic Enjoyment

Golf courses are often set in picturesque locations, allowing you to enjoy the beauty of nature while playing. It combines a leisurely walk in a park with a challenging sport.

Family Bonding

Golf can be a family affair. It's an excellent way for parents, grandparents, and children to spend quality time together. It's a family picnic with a fun, competitive twist.

Timeless Challenge

Golf is timeless. Its appeal doesn't diminish with age. As you gain experience, your understanding of the game deepens, and you appreciate its complexities even more.

Healthy Competition

Golf offers a healthy dose of competition. Whether competing against others or trying to beat your best score, it provides accomplishment and motivation. Everyone can be a winner.

Golf is a lifetime sport offering physical, mental, and social benefits. It adapts to your changing needs and abilities, ensuring it remains an enjoyable and rewarding activity as you grow older. So, whether you're a young beginner golfer or a seasoned player, golf can be a lifelong companion throughout your life journey.

Helpful Tips for Young Golfers

Regular Practice: Encourage regular practice sessions at the driving range or putting green. Consistency helps improve skills and fitness.

Stay Active Off the Course: Engage in physical activities like biking, swimming, or other sports to build fitness and endurance.

Balanced Diet: Eat a balanced diet with plenty of fruits, vegetables, lean proteins, and whole grains to support energy and growth.

Stay Hydrated: Drink water before, during, and after golf rounds to stay hydrated, especially on hot days.

Stretching: Incorporate stretching exercises to maintain flexibility and prevent injuries.

Strength Training: Develop strength with age-appropriate exercises to improve golf swings and fitness.

Warm-up: Before hitting the course, warm up with light jogging or jumping jacks to prepare muscles and joints.

Sun Protection: Use sunscreen, wear a hat, and protect the eyes with sunglasses to guard against harmful sun rays.

Proper Gear: Ensure that your golf clubs are the right size and that your golf shoes provide good traction for stability.

Listen to the Body: Teach children to listen to their bodies. If something doesn't feel right, take a break, or seek guidance from a coach or parent.

Mental Focus: Encourage mental focus and concentration, as golf requires physical and mental skills.

Safety First: Stress the importance of golf course safety, including awareness of other golfers and respecting course rules.

Have Fun: Keep the focus on enjoyment and not only competition. Golf should be fun and rewarding.

Set Goals: Help children set achievable goals for their golf game, fostering motivation and self-improvement.

By following these tips, young golfers can stay active and healthy and continually improve their golf skills while enjoying the sport to the fullest.

Chapter 8: The Joy of Golf

On the surface, it seems easy to play golf. All you have to do is put a shiny, white ball in a tiny, dark hole with the help of a sturdy, long stick. How you do that is entirely up to you, as long as you follow all the rules. You must put the ball in the cup before your opponent does. So, what makes golf interesting to play? Is it the technique of swinging the club that brings a smile to the players' faces? Or is it the game itself that fascinates them to no end? The truth is, it's a combination of these factors and then some.

    The joy of golf lies in the smell of the freshly mown grass on the early morning course, the goosebumps of anticipation crawling up your arms as you adjust the ball on the tee, and the feel of the air on your palm as you hold it up to judge the wind direction. Experience the thrill coursing through your veins when you raise your 7-iron high behind you, ready to take a swing. Cherish your sigh of relief as you hear the club head connecting perfectly with the ball, sending it soaring high and far, and feel the sweet taste of victory when it lands within a few taps of where you want it on the fairway.

    The satisfaction of getting your first perfect tee-off cannot compare to anything else. It's how Katharine Hepburn must have felt when she won her first Oscar in 1933 or Albert Einstein's eureka moments in the early 1900s when his relativity theories took shape. These moments are rare, so don't forget to capture your first perfect drive in your mind's eye because you will keep referring to it as your game progresses. Other popular reasons why golf will bring joy in your life are:

- **Socializing with People from All Walks of Life**

Golf is one of the very few sports games that can be enjoyed by both children and adults. Barely any exertion is involved, so the youngest of the young and the oldest of the old can play it. Did you know that Tiger Woods was recorded making a spectacular tee-off at the tender age of two?

No matter your age, you can find and socialize with people from all walks of life on your nearest golf course. Your grandmother will be as capable of playing the game as your kid brother. Golf is a great way to spend time with your family and friends from any generation.

23. *Golf is a great way to spend time with your family and friends from any generation. Source: https://pixabay.com/photos/golfers-group-photo-men-golf-clubs-960917/*

Making new friends on the course is easy. Are you new to the game? Ask for tips from the more experienced golfers around you. Are you fairly experienced? Lend your expertise to the novices in the field. Your socializing opportunities are endless.

- **Possibility to Compete with Anyone**

While your golf skills matter in a game, the handicap system makes it possible for you to compete with anyone on the course, regardless of how good or bad they are. Your golf handicap is the average number of strokes over par you can shoot. However, you must play quite a few games to determine your handicap. Here's how to calculate your handicap:

1. Pick your eight best scores from the previous 20 games you played.
2. Add those scores and divide the number by eight.

This number becomes your average number of strokes you need to add to the par of course you are playing on. Using your handicap, you can play competitively with a golfer of any expertise level.

- **Admiring the Great Outdoors**

Golf courses are usually constructed on scenic landscapes. It might be a vast stretch of grassy land surrounded by an extensive thicket of lush green trees or a never-ending set of rolling plains bordered with gargantuan silhouettes of snow-capped mountains. If you wish to admire the great outdoors while playing, there's no better game to play than golf.

Enjoying Different Types of Golf

Stroke Play

If you have already tried out golf, you might have only been practicing your drives and strokes. It's a great start. However, if you want to play a scoring game, there's no better way to begin than stroke play. It's a simple scoring system where you count the number of strokes it took for 18 holes. You can increase the number of rounds. The player with the lowest number of strokes wins the game. Four rounds are played on an 18-hole golf course in the US Open.

Match Play

Match play is played in the World Golf Championship (WGC). The number of strokes isn't counted in match play. You get a point for every hole you beat your opponent. The player with the most points at the end of all the rounds wins the game.

Scramble

A fun team game is Scramble. Two teams of four or two players each are formed. Each player in your team will tee off. You must choose the ball with the best drive, the one that reaches the furthest on the fairway or the rough. Choose a different ball for the putt or a different approach. Whichever team has the best score after putting in the cup wins the game.

Once you get the hang of the above three golf games, try more advanced games like the Chapman, Four-Ball Golf, Alternate Shot, and mixed format games.

Famous Junior Golfers

Pro golfers come in all sizes and ages. Pick any top junior golfer today and watch their game to hone and refine your golf skills. Are you looking for inspiration to play golf? Here are a few motivational stories of a few of the most famous junior golfers in the game's history.

- **Tiger Woods**

You must have guessed this name was bound to be on the list soon after reading the section's title. Tiger Woods inspired an entire generation of young sportspersons (not only golfers), aspiring and established, in his heyday. He put golf on the map. Children who had never heard of golf started playing with makeshift clubs and balls (any ball but a golf ball) all over the world in the late 1980s and '90s.

Woods was a child prodigy who might have shown his skills to the world at the age of two, but he started practicing the game way before that. Having a single-digit handicap golfer, Earl Woods, for a father also helped.

24. Woods was a child prodigy who might have shown his skills to the world at the age of two. Source: Keith Allison from Hanover, MD, USA, CC BY-SA 2.0 <https://creativecommons.org/licenses/by-sa/2.0>, via Wikimedia Commons: https://commons.wikimedia.org/wiki/File:Tiger_Woods_2018.jpg

- **Don Dunkelberger**

Despite starting to play golf at a tender age, it took 19 more years for Tiger Woods to become a pro golfer. Guess the age at which Don Dunkelberger turned pro? He was only 11 years of age. He is considered the youngest pro golfer of all time. He even reached the tournament level, but his career lost steam afterward.

- **Ariya Jutanugarn**

Ariya, the Thai golfer, was the same age as Dunkelberger (when he turned pro) when she qualified for the Ladies Professional Golf Association (LPGA) event. At 11 years old, she was the youngest player to qualify for the competition. She turned pro at 17, and four years later, she won the British Open, a women's major golf championship.

25. Ariya was the youngest player to qualify for the Ladies Professional Golf Association (LPGA) event. Source: Keith Allison from Hanover, MD, USA, CC BY-SA 2.0 <https://creativecommons.org/licenses/by-sa/2.0>, via Wikimedia Commons: https://commons.wikimedia.org/wiki/File:Moriya_Jutanugarn_2 017.jpg

- **Ben Hogan**

If you have followed golf's history, you are bound to know about Ben Hogan. He was among the first golfers to introduce swinging the ball in the game. He did not start playing as early as most other golfers due to a difficult childhood. His father committed suicide when he was nine years old. Despite his traumatic childhood, he took up golf at 14, focused on his game, and became a pro golfer three years later.

Setting Goals and Having Fun

All the junior golfers mentioned had one thing in common. They had set ambitious yet achievable goals for themselves and later went on to break their own expectations. It's time for you to do the same. So, start by setting a few realistic goals:

- **Aim Lower**

As you might know, the lower your golf handicap, the better your game. However, it doesn't mean you should directly aim for a scratch (0 handicap). Target the number a little lower than your current handicap. For instance, if you are 20 right now, aim for 18 within three months.

- **Play a New Type of Golf Each Year**

It's great if you're focusing on your stroke play, but switch it up a bit if your drives and putts have become decent enough. Play a new golf type, focusing on your other skills. Challenge yourself to master one different golf game variant each year.

- **Keep Track**

Keep constant track of your progress. Even if you play for fun, tracking your progress helps improve your game so that you can have even more fun with the complicated games.

It's perfectly okay if you don't achieve all your goals. Golf is a game of patience and perseverance. You will achieve your targets the next month. If not, there's always another month.

Conclusion

As you turn to the last page of this book, take a moment and pat yourself on the back. You've taken the first step in your lifelong journey of golfing adventures, and while many might disregard the theory, it lays the groundwork for perfecting the sport. This book is not only about hitting the ball into a hole. It's about fostering a love for the game and building skills to help you on and off the course. Its aim isn't merely to teach golf. It is to inspire a lifelong passion for this beautiful sport. Take a moment to review all you have learned so far. If at any point things seem confusing, head back to the particular section and refresh your memory.

You've learned it all, from understanding the history and significance of golf to mastering the fine details of golf swing, putting, and short game. Your journey through this book has equipped you with the skills necessary to succeed on a golf course and has instilled the discipline, etiquette, and rules that make young golfers like you the respected sportsperson of tomorrow.

Fairways, bunkers, and tees might have seemed strange terms at one point, but now you're familiar with them and understand how to navigate your way out of obstacles and look great doing it.

Throughout this book, the emphasis has been on the idea that golf is not only a sport but a lifelong journey filled with camaraderie, self-improvement, and achievement. The message to young golfers is to approach the game with patience, practice, a positive mentality, and an understanding that every shot, whether on the course or in life, is an opportunity to learn and grow.

As you come to the end of this book, remember what you've learned and embark on your golfing adventures. Practice, play, and enjoy the wonderful world of golf. Share experiences with others and remember the values of respect, honesty, and perseverance this game teaches.

Review and feedback on this book are highly appreciated because they help young golfers like you to tee off on a lifetime of enjoyment and success in the game of golf. Thank you for becoming a part of this journey, and here's a last-minute tip before you head off to the golf course. Keep this book next to your clubs. When you're stuck in a bunker, open the book, and you'll find a handy tip to help you get out of the sandy traps.

References

(N.d.). Usga.org. https://www.usga.org/content/usga/home-page/rules-hub/topics/bunkers.html#:~:text=Bunkers%20are%20one%20of%20the,ball%20is%20in%20a%20bunker.

10 basic tips that can help golfers chip better than ever. (2021, May 31). Golf. https://golf.com/instruction/short-game/10-tips-golfer-chipping-better-than-ever/

10 reasons your kids should play golf. (2021, December 21). Indian River Golf Foundation. https://irgf.org/10-reasons-your-kids-should-play-golf/

15 simple, quick ways to calm nerves at work. (2023, August 16). Calmer. https://www.thisiscalmer.com/blog/how-to-calm-nerves-at-work

5 easy steps to get up and down from the bunker like a pro. (2021, March 4). Golf. https://golf.com/instruction/bunker-shots/how-to-hit-bunker-shot-five-tips/

6 things junior golfers (and their parents) need to know about golf equipment. (2020, December 23). Golf. https://golf.com/gear/6-things-junior-golfers-need-know-golf-equipment/

9 benefits of introducing your children to the sport of golf - the cliffs. (2022, August 5). The Cliffs | Private Luxury Communities In South and North Carolina; The Cliffs. https://cliffsliving.com/blog/activities/golf-best-sport-for-kids/

Charlie. (2019, April 9). Green reading: Unlocking the mystery. The Left Rough. https://theleftrough.com/reading-greens/

Charlie. (2020, February 4). Golf Sun Protection: 11 Tips to save your skin. The Left Rough. https://theleftrough.com/golf-sun-protection/

Charlie. (2021, December 28). Actual helpful advice: The best golf tips for kids. The Left Rough. https://theleftrough.com/best-golf-tips-for-kids/

Charlie. (2021, May 21). Golf clubs for kids: Set your child up for success in golf. The Left Rough. https://theleftrough.com/best-golf-clubs-for-kids/

Charlie. (2023, February 20). More than stroke play: The different types of golf games & formats. The Left Rough. https://theleftrough.com/types-of-golf-games/

Dingledine, R. (2022, January 10). Kids golf: 8 steps to teach your kids to play and love golf. Golf Guidebook. https://golfguidebook.com/kids-golf-teach-your-kids-golf/

Dingledine, R. (2022, January 14). Setting golf goals: 4 tips to become A better player. Golf Guidebook. https://golfguidebook.com/golf-goals/

Drobnjak, L. (2014, June 12). 5 fun golf games for kids - gross motor activities. The Inspired Treehouse. https://theinspiredtreehouse.com/gross-motor-activities-golf-games-for-kids/

Eaton, V. (2022, February 24). 8 Youngest Pro Golfers in history. Oldest.org. https://www.oldest.org/sports/youngest-pro-golfers/

Ellis, P. (2023, June 28). Unlock your potential: Expert-Recommended Golf Drills for junior golf practice routines. Noisy Golf; Noisy Golf Ltd. https://noisygolf.com/junior-golf-coaching/unlock-your-potential-expert-recommended-golf-drills-for-junior-golf-practice-routines/

Geddis, T., Alberstadt, B., & Magliocco, G. (2021, December 4). A guide to buying junior golf equipment. Golfwrx.com. https://www.golfwrx.com/665827/a-guide-to-buying-junior-golf-equipment/

Golf gear for kids: Our top picks. (n.d.). Golfing Focus. https://golfingfocus.com/recommended-gear-my-picks/golf-gear-for-kids-our-top-picks/

Golf scoring terms (par, bogey, birdie, eagle, albatross, and more). (n.d.). GolfBit. https://golfbit.com/golf-scoring-terms

Golf swing basics: The fundamentals you need to know. (2020, March 19). The Left Rough. https://theleftrough.com/golf-swing-basics/

Golf swing tips. (2018, February 15). Golf Distillery. https://www.golfdistillery.com/swing-tips/

Golf, M. (2021, October 28). How to select golf clubs for kids. Haggin Oaks; Morton Golf. https://www.hagginoaks.com/blog/how-to-select-golf-clubs-for-kids/

Golf. (n.d.). In Encyclopedia Britannica.

Golfers, H. (2021, September 15). What is a Putt (in Golf Terms)? Honest Golfers. https://honestgolfers.com/what-is-a-putt-in-golf-terms/

Hay, G. (2019, July 11). What is fun about golf? 5 reasons it really is. Golfing Focus. https://golfingfocus.com/golf-fun-really-5-reasons-why-it-really-is/

Heidelberger, N. (n.d.). What is the Tee Box in Golf? Golflink.com; GolfLink. https://www.golflink.com/golf-rules/what-is-the-tee-box-in-golf

Hercules, A. (2022, September 22). How to tee off in golf for beginners? Hit consistent tee shots. Flawless Golf. https://flawlessgolf.com/how-to-tee-off-in-golf-for-beginners/

How to choose the right golf club for you. (2018, April 16). Golf Drives. https://www.golf-drives.com/guides/choosing-golf-clubs/

How to get started playing golf with your kids. (2021, July 21). RUN WILD MY CHILD. https://runwildmychild.com/golfing-with-kids/

In-depth guide to mastering your golf pitch shots. (n.d.). BombTech Golf. https://www.bombtechgolf.com/blogs/news/what-golf-pitch-wedge-shots-difference-chip

Kelley, B. (2003, August 27). Here's why a Par-3 course is great for beginning golfers. LiveAbout. https://www.liveabout.com/what-is-a-par-3-course-1560945

Kids Golf Training and Practice - Tips and exercises. (2020, January 5). Golf Today. https://golftoday.co.uk/kids-golf-training-and-practice/

Livesay, J. (2022, September 3). How does a golf handicap work? Here's how to calculate your own in a few steps. USA Today. https://www.usatoday.com/story/sports/golf/2022/09/03/how-to-calculate-golf-handicap/10175044002/

Metz, M. (2006, August 30). How to swing a golf club. WikiHow. https://www.wikihow.com/Swing-a-Golf-Club

Parker, L. (2023, May 16). What is A fairway in golf? Essential guide to mastering the game. SunriseGolf.Co. https://sunrisegolf.co/blog/what-is-a-fairway-in-golf/

Powers, C. (2018, June 6). The 15 best golf practice games. GolfDigest. https://www.golfdigest.com/story/the-15-best-golf-practice-games

Preston, L. (2023, July 24). Introducing golf games for kids: Tips for a fun experience. Motherhood Diaries Parenting Magazine - Preconception Planning | Pregnancy Journal | Birth Stories. https://www.motherhooddiaries.com/introducing-golf-games-for-kids/

Preventing golf injuries. (n.d.). Rush.edu. https://www.rush.edu/news/preventing-golf-injuries

Rookie Road. (2021, April 11). Golf basic rules for kids. Rookieroad.com; Rookie Road. https://www.rookieroad.com/golf/basic-rules-for-kids/

Rookie Road. (2021, April 11). Golf basic rules for kids. Rookieroad.com; Rookie Road. https://www.rookieroad.com/golf/basic-rules-for-kids/

Shaw, W. (2021, February 21). Golf grip: How to hold A golf club. Golf Insider UK. https://golfinsideruk.com/how-to-hold-golf-club-proper-golf-grip/

Stevens, M. (2022, July 12). 11 often overlooked reasons why golf is actually fun. Golf Workout Program. https://golfworkoutprogram.com/golf-is-fun/

Tips On Teaching Kids Proper Golf Etiquette. (2018, January 10). AussieKids Golf Academy. https://aussiekids.com/tips-on-teaching-kids-proper-golf-etiquette/

Top reasons children should golf - golf lessons for kids. (2019, August 21). Colonial Golf & Tennis -. https://colonialgolftennis.com/blog/reasons-children-should-play-golf/

U.S. kids golf. (n.d.). Uskidsgolf.com. https://www.uskidsgolf.com/

What do golf tee marker colors mean? (2023, June 14). From Tee To Green. https://www.fromteetogreen.com/post/tee-marker-colors

Williams, V. (2018, April 16). How to teach your junior golfer the full swing. Golf Tips Magazine -; Golf Tips Magazine. https://www.golftipsmag.com/instruction/full-swing/junior-golfer-full-swing

Made in the USA
Monee, IL
02 June 2025